Beyond The Technique: an exploration of artistry & authenticity

Susan Eichhorn Young

Published by SEY Voice LLC, 2024.

While every precaution has been taken in the preparation of this book, the publisher assumes no responsibility for errors or omissions, or for damages resulting from the use of the information contained herein.

BEYOND THE TECHNIQUE: AN EXPLORATION OF ARTISTRY & AUTHENTICITY

First edition. June 20, 2024.

Copyright © 2024 Susan Eichhorn Young.

ISBN: 979-8990654211

Written by Susan Eichhorn Young.

Table of Contents

Prelude 1
What Brings You Here? 3
The Artist Mindset 7
Authentic Voice | What is authenticity? 11
Claiming Your Authentic Voice 15
What Does it Mean, Physically? 19
Beyond, but.. 23
Technique? Sexy?... 25
Commitment.. 29
Lost in Translation 33
A Winding Path 37
The Psyche & Mindset | The Choosing 39
Process or Product Mindset 43
Longevity 47
The Power of Language 51
Reinvention 55
The Artist 59
Magic... 61
Abracadabra & Audacity 65
Artistic Energy 69
The Essential Artist 73
Remaining Unapologetic 77
The Craft 79
Get Ready, Be Ready, Stay Ready 81
Practicing Craft 83
The Secret of Craft 87
What Is in the Control of Craft? 89
What Ever Happened to Craft? 93
Postlude | Play!.. 97
Glitter & Unicorn Poop.. 99

What People Are Saying...

Susan has written a book that is a valuable resource for all singers, no matter what their path of study. It is about more than singing. It is about finding your authentic voice with vulnerability and courage. I can't recommend it highly enough!
   Linda Dahl, MD
   Professional Voice Doctor for Broadway, television, and film
   www.drlindadahl.com[1]

This book is so informative and thought provoking! It is making me take a very close look at how, why, and what I choose to sing. It is a guidebook for anyone who uses their voice - whether it be for singing, speaking, teaching, professionals, or amateurs!
   Lillias White, Multi Award-Winning Actor/Singer

"At a time when much of our work, as artists/performers, is driven by commercialism, it is essential to define ourselves by the peculiar rhythms we create. Self expression should never be overdetermined by what we are willing to do for outside recognition. Such self examination distinguishes the artist who wrestles for authenticity and such distinction fulfills those who constantly asks, "is the juice worth the squeeze?" This book invites all of us to venture into this crucial self examination. Every reading and re-reading reveals another truth about the self and the relationship to one's own concept of authenticity."
   Keith David, Multi-Award-Winning Actor, Singer

---

1. http://www.drlindadahl.com

I love collaborating with Susan to take care of singers from all walks of life, at all experience levels – so it is a joy to read this inspiring text – no, love letter – to singers, infused with joy and wonder at the magic of singing, and informed with deep knowledge of the hard work that undergirds it. These reflections and exhortations from a teacher who has guided so many, so faithfully and passionately – they are ideal cues to singers honing their craft and finding their authentic voices.

Dr Paul E. Kwak, MD
Laryngology & Voice, Otolaryngology, NYU Langone

"Susan Eichhorn Young is a light of a human being and a talent. She has encouraged, healed, and inspired hundreds of Artists across the country and around the world - from movie stars to Broadway luminaries, to everyday people who want to pursue their bliss as singers and storytellers. Susan's techniques are pure GOLD, and this book will become a "North Star" for Artists of all ages for years to come."

Will Nunziata, Award-winning Director

"Beyond the Technique" is an indispensable guide for any performing artist embarking on a journey towards mastery. With its insightful questions and thought-provoking reflection sections, this book cultivates a mindset of growth, self-discovery, and artistic evolution all while gently reminding artists of the joy of play."

Christine Schneider
The Visceral Voice, Manual Voice and Biomechanics Specialist

"I read the words "what brings you here?" and a shiver went down my spine. This book, truly in Susan's voice, strikes the perfect pitch of spirituality and practicality. The book defines questions, yet leaves room for you, the artist, to define your own questions.

James T Lane, award-winning singer/actor/dancer

"Susan creates a safe space not only for her students, but now readers too, who can have opinions through their own unique lens and bring that authenticity to the raw talent and intricate technique of being a singer. The marriage of the voice to the body and spirit is a gift that is priceless and infinite."

David Burtka, Actor, Singer, Chef

"A powerful, straight forward guide and companion, Beyond the Technique, gives all artists (no matter where you are in your career) permission to get out of their own way and find their unique voice. Focusing on the things we can control -developing our talent, craft and mindset-this book keeps you in the conversation that is necessary for the work and play that is an artistic life. I'll be recommending this to all my students. "

Matthew Corozine, Author "If You Survived 7th Grade, You Can Be An Actor."

Founding Artistic Director/Acting Coach Matthew Corozine Acting Studio and Theatre (MCS)

"We have known Susan Eichhorn Young for over 2 decades, first as mentors, now as friends and colleagues. We have always been amazed at her instinct regarding what it takes to be a successful person and performer at the same time. This book exemplifies what she lives, herself: The practical, caring, and logical way of approaching the development of one's gifts. We would say to any singer or performer; Read, act, and believe! Thank you, Susan, for sharing this with all of us in such a meaningful way."

Irena Welhasch Baerg, Internationally Renowned Soprano
Theodore Baerg, Internationally Renowned Baritone
Professor of Voice, Director - Opera Western, Western University

"The way you do one thing is the way you do everything, and Susan makes it clear from the beginning that her approach goes beyond the vocals to give you an all encompassing technique for life as an artist. Susan gives you techniques for how to check-in, reveal, and respond to yourself. She shows you how to engage with your unique creative process while giving permission to let it look and feel however it's meant to, for you. She highlights the power of simplicity and reminds us that big change comes from small shifts in awareness. Susan guides you to ask questions without needing the answer, to remain open to your intuition and trust all is revealed in perfect timing. This is a salve to the artistic soul and battlecry for creating authentic success in a world that doesn't understand it. You will undoubtedly learn the art of honing your authentically sexy voice, but your life may just be transformed in tandem, beyond the technique."

Jenn Lederer, Comedian and Keynote Speaker

"*Beyond the Technique* is about finding your voice: pedagogically, artistically, and commercially. It celebrates authenticity, integrity, and the symbiotic relationship between craft and business acumen.

Susan's wisdom comes from being a veteran performer in a multi-generational artistic family, a career balanced between singing and teaching, and decades as a consultant, clinician, writer, and more. There's a "No B.S." approach from surviving a near-death experience and understanding the glitter and grit of show business from supporting working artists daily.

Wherever you are in your voice journey, or life as an artist, allow Susan to speak to you. She illuminates the holistic nature of artistic expression encompassing mind, body, and soul – bridging physical and spiritual realms. She doesn't profess to have all the answers. Instead, she shares her knowledge and experience and provides you with lists upon lists of incredible questions.

Pick it up and play... write to uncover answers in your own voice and truth. Clear the channel and discover confidence from the power of your unique voice. Go make waves!"

Tony Howell, Brand Strategist

"This is a fantastic guide for navigating the mental and emotional process of getting to know YOUR voice and what to look for when seeking a voice teacher or coach. The reader takes an active role in the book's journey toward authenticity and vocal freedom. Susan successfully identifies and validates the challenges and emotions experienced when a singer/performer/creator explores their voice and career."

Eddie Schnecker - Vocal Coach/LMSW

"Susan Eichhorn Young's book is a profound exploration of the artist's journey, delving deep into the essence of creativity and self-expression. From the foundational questions of purpose and mindset to the intricate nuances of authenticity and craft, each chapter offers invaluable insights and practical wisdom. Susan' eloquent prose and thought-provoking reflections guide readers through the labyrinth of artistic endeavor, inspiring them to claim their authentic voice, embrace commitment, and navigate the winding path of creativity with courage and resilience. With its blend of introspection and inspiration, this book is an indispensable companion for anyone seeking to unlock their creative potential and embrace the magic of artistic expression."

Othalie Graham, world-renowned dramatic soprano

"*Beyond the Technique* is the most interactive book on singing that I have ever read. Susan Eichhorn-Young takes the singer on a personal journey of self-discovery, peeling away layers of expectations, fears, and influences to help the artist find the true essence of their individual voices. This book will help the artist embrace vulnerability and sing from the gut without inhibition. I wish this book had been around when I started learning to sing. It takes a long time to find one's authentic voice but Beyond the Technique will get you there faster. I highly recommend this book!"

Marcus Nance, Operatic & Broadway Bass-baritone/Voice Teacher

"Susan possesses a depth of knowledge, depth of heart, and depth of intuition that is rare. She expertly balances concrete steps with magic and presents it all with a lightness of spirit, vulnerability, and a sense of humor. The Reflections are such a great place to absorb the ideas into practice, and perhaps help readers to shift their lens to something they've not considered before! She is an expert at excavating artistry

"Beyond the Technique" because she has lived it, cultivated it in herself, and been teaching it to students for many years. This book is written with true love and respect for the reader."

Cara Lianne McLeod, soprano, singer/songwriter

Beyond the Technique is, quite frankly, a breath of fresh air. Susan is not only a master voice technician and mentor, she's a fierce advocate for artists who is unafraid to ask the hard questions — she's unafraid to encourage the artist to delve deep into self-exploration and get curious (and honest!) with ourselves.

Susan speaks candidly about the singer's mindset, artistry, authenticity, and approach in a way that feels like an intimate conversation over a good cup of coffee. At the end of each chapter, Susan asks thought provoking questions that encourage us to look deeper into each topic to examine our "why" and our artistic process.

I HIGHLY recommend Susan's book to any singer/actor who wants to deepen their understanding of their artistry and cultivate a thriving relationship with their voice.

Kelly Slawson, Dramatic Soprano

DEDICATION

To my Dad, Archie Eichhorn.
He was, and will always remain my father, and my North Star.
He was a Renaissance Man: A teacher, a director, a producer, a painter, a creative, an artist. He taught me to think, to be, to ask questions, to laugh at myself, to feel and express through music, art, writing, and stage.
Thank you, Dad, for seeing me, nurturing me, and mentoring me. Thank you for believing in me and loving me without hesitation and without condition. It's because of you that I am here. This is part of your prolific legacy. I love you always.

Thank you!

Where do I begin?

I have been writing my entire life - filling notebooks and binders in cursive (because I am that many years old) of fiction, poetry, plays and musings.

There are so many that I must thank, and so if I forget someone, know you are in my consciousness somewhere!

First, to my editor, Katy Lindhart, who has incredible insight, foresight and humor and means the world to me. This would not have happened without you, and I adore you!!!

Thank you to Tony Howell: you gave me the title of this book YEARS ago and you remain an integral and essential part of my inner circle.

To my husband, Thomas, for an eternity of support and love and belief in me.

To my daughter, Erin, for her consistent fierceness, honesty, and love; for always having my back and being the best human barometer, a momma could ask for.

To my family, both blood & chosen, for growing with me and keeping me grounded.

To the teachers and mentors throughout my life: I thank you for all you do, and you know who you are. Thank you for the lessons you have taught me. I have learned so much.

To my students and clients, over all these years, who have taught me more than I could ever teach you. You are why I teach.

And finally, to you, dear reader, for picking this up, or downloading it onto your device. I am honored and humbled that you would take the time to read and explore this book. I hope it can be of service in the smallest of ways as you journey through your authenticity and artistry.

With much fondness and appreciation,
Susan

Forward
From Katy Lindhart, Editor

If you're reading this, you're probably a singer, and a devoted one at that. And thank goodness, because now I don't have to explain to you all the mental, physical, and plain old logistical complications that come with our chosen art form.

And it's really never-ending, isn't it? Just when you think you've gotten your technique down, your hormones shift a millimeter and you've got to relearn the last 15 years. Just when you think you've got a handle on the psychology of Mrs. Lovett or are beginning to understand what Lucia's mad scene really means to you, life experience comes along and rocks your reality. As artists—and as human beings—we are always learning and constantly evolving. It's a natural part of our life cycle, whether we like it or not, so we might as well enjoy discovering who we are.

It's not easy to embrace our own authentic artistry, because it involves embracing ourselves. For many of us, that goes against everything we've been taught. We're hearing what we're supposed to look like, act like, and sound like from a hundred different messengers at any given moment. In the face of all that, authenticity feels radical. It might even feel downright terrifying (that's because it is).

A perfect singing technique is all well and good, but without authenticity, it falls flat. At the same time, an authentic voice without a semblance of technique is admirable, but without technique, no one will be interested in listening to it. True artistry requires a mastery of both. The work you do to merge craft and authenticity is what will allow your artistry to blossom and grow. The two go hand in hand.

Susan taught me that. And now she's here to guide you on the same journey.

You're in good hands.

What are you looking for?

If you are looking for a book about vocal technique, this isn't it.

Instead, this is a book for you, the performer, the artist, to look beyond, beneath, around, and above. This book is meant to help you, to challenge you, to uncover what is within.

Artistic work is never finished, and it is rarely linear. We move, we morph, we circle back, we re-visit and explore, always learning and allowing in new insight and observations into our now.

This book is set up to do the same: you don't need to necessarily read it or explore it from beginning to end. You can discover sections that resonate with you in any order you wish, and return.

The space between the artist and the teacher should be collaborative: combining truths, reflections, creating safety to explore. It is not to please, but to reveal and claim the alchemy of vibrational tangibility and creative process. It is the mutual trust that allows the magic to occur, because if you cannot release into a space of safety & trust, how do you truly create?

This moment is our "now." It is our "beyond." Sit down beside me, exhale, get curious, and let's explore together!

You will find questions to reflect on and observe throughout the book. Do not let that intimidate you. They are there IF you want it. Grab a notebook or journal and MUSE!

ALL of your thoughts & experiences are valid. Returning to your reflections again and again can reveal growth, and moments of clarity. Use it however it makes sense to you.

This is YOUR journey. This is YOUR book: get messy and color outside the lines!

Prelude

"Art, in itself, is an attempt to bring order out of chaos.[2]" - Stephen Sondheim

---

2. https://www.azquotes.com/quote/277750

"I think everything in life is art. What you do. How you dress. The way you love someone, and how you talk. Your smile and your personality. What you believe in, and all your dreams. The way you drink your tea. How you decorate your home. Or party. Your grocery list. The food you make. How your writing looks. And the way you feel. Life is art."- Helena Bonham Carter

What Brings You Here?

When a singer books an initial consultation to see if we might work together in the studio, one of my first questions is: What brings you here? So, as you begin this book, I ask the same question.

There is no correct or incorrect answer. There is simply YOUR answer.

The answers range from very vague, to very specific, to somewhere in-between. You might not know why. That's okay. You may think you know why, and perhaps that is the initial stimulus to get you there, but the why will change as you begin to explore. That's okay too.

I don't ask that question to cause angst, or to try to trick you. It's not a trick question.

Your answer helps me find you where you are, or where you seem to be. This gives us both a clearer understanding about how and why you entered this space, and where you might be going.

That's a lot, isn't it? Did you realize how much is going on with that initial question? And, perhaps, how much is going on in your answer?

This is the psyche, the conscious and the unconscious and preconscious guiding simultaneously.

Questions don't have to be overwhelming, but sometimes, the answers seem to be.

When you decide to make something happen—sign up for a class, contact a teacher or a coach, plan to record a reel, go to an audition, pick up a book (!)—do you take that moment of stillness to ask yourself: "What brings me here?"

Think about it. What brought you to this point? What motivated you to arrive at this decision?

Often the answers will be vague, or generic. That's okay. Sometimes they need to be, in order for you to simply take the step forward and into the space your psyche is coaxing you.

Sometimes, the answers will be full of excuses. That's okay too. It's a protection mechanism in order for you to feel safe as you make a decision before you take what might feel like a leap.

Sometimes, the answers will be very specific, based on what you know and realize and recognize. Those answers will change as you begin to allow your consciousness and subconsciousness time to collaborate!

You don't need to get creative with your answer. Sometimes the most mundane answer is the truest! The truth of that answer, conscious or not, allows you to come closer to why you come to the studio/space/ insert location here; what brings you there; what can be done while you are there; and what could be possible after you leave.

Here's the deal: you don't have to do anything. The "have to" creates angst, resistance, excuses, or delusion. You need none of that.

You may choose to do something for a reason that makes sense to you. If that reason is something that resonates with the space you want to walk into, then you can explore more of what can be done in that space to develop more specificity in your journey. You don't have to explain it. You simply can begin to explore it.

"What brings you here?" has the power and the potential to reveal the authenticity of you in the moment. It also has the power to pivot you to "what can we do?" and "how do we achieve that?" and "what needs our attention first?".

"What brings you here?" can reveal whether you are first and foremost a big picture person or detail oriented. Often it is a little of both.

The beauty of the question is that the answer can remain fluid until you have that lucid and conscious "a-ha!" moment that gives you tangibility. Then you can simply act upon it.

Nothing is random unless we are unwilling or unable to commit.

As an artist (or someone with an artistic temperament), we have the imagination to create possibilities. In doing so, we can focus them into a very specific and tangible format.

So, what brings you here? Trust that if you don't know, you will find out by asking the question and being open enough to observe the answer before acting!

REFLECTIONS TO MUSE UPON...

What made you pick up this book?

What are you hoping to discover or realize while reading & working through the reflections?

The Artist Mindset

There is a great deal of difference between being an artist and being an artist trying to make a living in the business.

In the studio, when I ask the question, "Why are you here?" The performer who is not motivated by artistry but rather by business will answer with "I need to work, I want a job, I have to be working before the end of the summer, I need to book a gig."

The artist will answer differently. The artist wants the craft, wants the knowledge, wants to tell a story, and wants to reveal a truth.

Then there are those who are wanting both but direct them in opposite directions.

Now, don't get me wrong, artists that are in the business must learn to think from a business perspective. But it is not the first thing that enters their minds. The artistic spirit has difficulty entering the business mind. They simply do not function in their day-to-day life with that "hire me NOW" mentality. They want to make beautiful music. They want to show a journey through storytelling. They want to discover a way to live that has depth, meaning, and beauty.

Business simply isn't thinking that way.

Being an artist in the business of show is an odd and bizarre dance. Sometimes it's hard to know what beats we are leaning into. Is it the two and the four, or is it the one and three?

Often, we look at who is working and, even though there might be talent there, we are puzzled by why such average talent/ability works while the true artist is often passed over. This is the million-dollar question (and before you get your panties in a twist, I am generalizing! But you know you've wondered too!). This isn't to say the "artist first" isn't working. It just means that that artist has had to create a mindset to stay flexible in the business world of show.

So, if you are an artistic soul, it is about how you live your life, not just what you do in your business. Your artistry is not just about the craft, but how you approach your day-to-day life in every way.

How do you reconcile this soul with the business? You want that business to recognize that artistry, that possibility, that "IT" factor that is often unspoken. Yet somehow you come up short. Sometimes, someone with less ability, less training, less passion, less something, gets the nod. WHY?!

Well, sadly, there are as many reasons as grains of sand. Trying to riddle this enigma out will drive you nuts. Truly.

So, how can we simplify??? What is the reality of the artist in the business?

How do you market yourself? What are you selling? How do you sell it?

Okay, those of you who are artists just threw up in your mouth a little - and I shuddered at it too. But guess what? This is the balance beam we walk each day if we choose to allow our artistic nature/spirit to inhabit our craft in order to pursue a career possibility.

If the word "marketing" or "branding" makes you itch, get creative and explore other ways of describing it to yourself. Often, I just ask "what do you want to REVEAL about yourself?"

When I say simplify, I mean it. Too much may not be too much for you, but it can be overwhelming in the business of auditioning, or submission.

You, as the artist mindset will always ask "seriously? That's IT?!" Yes, yes it is.

We often try to do too much in the room, say too much in a cover letter, and the list goes on. Think of it as a first date: just entice enough so you get asked out again!

Making a distinct choice of what you CHOOSE to reveal can be powerful.

It is not the business of artistry. Let me say that again: It is not the business of artistry.

Nothing is guaranteed. Nothing is promised. Be that artist, but then acknowledge that you are going to have to shift your mindset angle to allow that artist to try to make a living in the business of show.

When asked, "What do you want to do?" an artistic soul will speak from that. They want to be a better singer, a better self, to discover what they can sing well or how to tell a story.

Now, take that artistic desire to seek and put on the business hat. What do you need to show in order to do? How do you reconcile artist/performer/business and still sleep at night?

First and foremost, you do not need to sacrifice your artistic spirit. Ever. You simply need to recognize, understand, and develop the tools you aren't as familiar with. The product is you. What does the business need to see of you? To hear from you? To acknowledge immediately about you?

"Business hat" is not the same as "Artistic hat." Learning how to wear both— and when to wear one over the other—is the key. Perhaps it's the same hat, and just worn on a different angle.

Understanding and taking charge of when the artistic angle is needed, then recognizing when the business angle needs to be fully apparent is part of your marketing as an artist in the business of show. It's part of your survival. It's part of how you will thrive.

Show them what they need to see in order to get the job, the opportunity, the foot in the door. Then, your artistry can expand its wings and encompass the craft and journey you are meant to be a part of.

Craft is part of business. If you have none, or have limited access to it, the business will only offer you a moment. It will simply replace you if you cannot follow through.

Artistry is revealed when craft is built, and talent can be summoned at will to inhabit the space the business has invited you to enter.

Without the business, you are still an artist. You wake up as an artist, and you fall asleep as an artist. This gives you power, a sense of self, of purpose, of truth, no matter what.

If you are simply about business with no craft or artistry, you rely only on what the business acknowledges. That falls flat pretty quickly.

Believe, reconcile, and recognize what you are capable of doing, what you are actually doing, how you are doing it, and why you do it.

Ponder, Muse & Reflect

What motivates you first before all else?

What inspires you? Who inspires you? How does that inspiration present itself?

What gives you meaning on a day-to-day basis?

Where are you currently in your journey of "artist in the process of business"?

Where would you like to be?

Where do you NEED to be, and what do you need to DO to create that possibility a reality?

Authentic Voice
What is authenticity?

I ask this question regularly of myself and of the singers in my studio. I don't expect a definitive answer, because authenticity is constantly morphing and shifting and re-designing itself, but I will continue to explore the defining factors.

Brené Brown defines it this way, and this resonates with me:

"To be authentic, we must cultivate the courage to be imperfect — and vulnerable. We have to believe that we are fundamentally worthy of love and acceptance, just as we are. I've learned that there is no better way to invite more grace, gratitude, and joy into our lives than by mindfully practicing authenticity."

Authenticity has so many layers, so many complexities, and so many possibilities. It is doing, it is being, it is a practice of action, and an action of practice. Authenticity is messy, it's curious, it's magnificent, and it's constantly changing.

#authenticvoice has been part of my brand for many years. It continues with the work I do in the studio, with my blog, and the presence I strive to create in the artistic community and beyond. It has become my purpose in my little corner of the world, and how it can matter there.

Authenticity creates true safety because there is integrity present.

Authenticity creates trust because there is genuine compassion present.

In our business of show, no matter what area you are in, we see the extremes and all the gray in between; the truly authentic, those striving to find authenticity, those pretending to be authentic, those wishing to be authentic, and the phony. We see and experience truth, and we see and experience falsehood, ignorance, and their darker cousins, arrogance, and fear, which perpetuate abuse and misuse.

The more we seek the authenticity of self, of craft, of our work, the more it reveals itself to us and through us. The more attuned we are with our own authentic selves, the less the other noise matters and the more we can change the space we inhabit. I am constantly questioning and seeking, and I don't believe anything is in a fixed state. If something is real, it must constantly be evolving in order to meet the complexities it reveals and acknowledges.

Authenticity has that quality. It is a living, breathing, continuing-to-evolve process within each of us. We must continue to reveal what is real and what is true - to ourselves primarily - in order for others to be touched by our authenticity in the room and from the stage. So, what does all this mean for you?

I cannot give you an absolute definition of authenticity, and I cannot tell you what your individual authenticity looks like. I can, however, offer you permission to keep exploring what it means to you; how it could reveal itself to you through your voice and your craft. If you need it, I can give you permission to live your life in a way that gives you purpose and clarity. I can encourage you to keep seeking, discovering, and evolving to live in whatever that authenticity is today. How you choose to share it in YOUR corner of the world is up to you.

Seek authenticity.
Question authenticity.
Practice authenticity.
Be authenticity.
It's not perfection, but it's certainly not beige!
Wherever you are, be there. Sometimes the location isn't ideal, but the authenticity of you in that space can salvage more than you realize. Whoever you are, be that. That being of you will evolve if you trust and stay present.

Nobody wants to sleepwalk through their life; at least I hope not. Discovering one's own authenticity is crucial to truly finding your purpose and adding meaning to everyday things, not just big-ticket items. Learn how to be present each day and each moment. Explore, make choices, get messy! All this is how you figure out "you."

Your authenticity awaits!

REFLECTIONS

When you hear the word "authenticity," what comes to your mind today? Create a list of word association: (come back to this question periodically to see what changes)

Who and/or what represents authenticity to you? Why?

Is there a behavior that represents authenticity to you? Where do you see that?

Claiming Your Authentic Voice

What is your authentic voice, both literally and figuratively, and how do you claim it?

I can tell you what it is not: it's not a cop-out. It's not an excuse. It's not a dismissal. It's not a place to hide. It's not a term to just throw around.

You cannot say "Well, that's just my authentic voice, I can't do anything about that," or "If they don't like me, it's not my fault, that's my authentic voice; I can't improve, develop, or grow, because that's just my authentic voice. That's just who I am."

Well, you could say that, but is that really authentic?

No. It's not (but you knew that already). That's the fear talking. That's the dismissal, the hiding-in-plain-sight talking.

The true authentic voice defies all of that. It demands your full attention, even if it's uncomfortable. Especially when it's uncomfortable.

Integrity is defined as "a firm adherence to a code of especially moral or artistic values; an unimpaired condition; the quality or state of being complete or undivided." Your authenticity not only mirrors your integrity; it illuminates it. It is more than being passionate about or committed to something. It is the being of it all. Integrity is big. It's real. It's serious. It's playful. It's the glue. It's everything.

Integrity guides from its moral compass. Authenticity breathes in the present tense. This is why authenticity and integrity dance together and reflect each other so magically.

Authenticity is discovered in your present, in your "now." In every now. As you move from now to now, you continue to discover more of what your individual authenticity means, how it is felt, how it projects, and how it lives—for you and within you.

The authentic voice morphs, develops, reveals, and embraces. It speaks precisely and directly in the present tense of who we are and where we are, not where we were, where we wish to be, or who we wish we were.

Your authentic voice is uniquely and magnificently YOU. All the beauty of you, all the messiness of you. It contains all your confusion and frustration, your experience, the laughter, the tears, the depression, the anxiety, the exhilaration, the excitement, the possibility! It reveals the half full glass, the half empty, or just that there is a glass. It is multidimensional and allows all things to co-exist at once.

Authenticity is full of complexity and yet feels like being completely home. It is claimed moment to moment in how you live and how you respond to the world within you and around you, not just in the audition room, the rehearsal space, or on the stage.

Authenticity is a huge responsibility, but remember, huge doesn't have to be heavy. It can be buoyant and pliable and elastic. We have the choice in determining how weighted that responsibility is, and who we share that with.

What is your authentic voice about right now? What could it reveal about you and your craft as you take a step into it?

Maybe it doesn't feel very authentic right now. That's okay too.

If we are leaning into the process of authentic voice through integrity, we will never say, "I have fully found my authentic voice." We may say, "I am beginning to claim what I am finding through my authentic voice" or "I am discovering what my authentic voice is revealing."

I AM my authentic voice. My authentic voice is ME. So, if you are saying, "I don't know what my authentic voice is..." then it is precisely the right time to take the first step. Let it begin to reveal itself as you pursue the discovery of this lifetime journey.

REFLECTIONS

What do I recognize as my authenticity today?
What would I want others to say about my authenticity?
How do I want to grow that authenticity?

*****Pay attention to the answers and how it feels in your body. Learning to trust your gut in these moments of claiming authenticity is crucial.

Come back to these questions daily, weekly, monthly to reveal more about YOUR authentic self to YOU.

What Does it Mean, Physically?

The pursuit of authenticity through voice is such an integral part of what I do, and how I teach. I strive to combine my knowledge, my studies, my ears, and my intuition to continue to find my own authenticity and where it leads me, as well as helping guide voices that come to work and explore.

On the surface, this may seem like a no-brainer, yet it is more complex than we might initially assume.

As it pertains to the literal voice, authenticity isn't just the physicality of the voice, but the actual motivation and intention behind it. The journey of authenticity illuminates the combination of discovering and integrating the tangibles with the intangibles, then establishing physical behavior. It then begins informing and creating intention.

This is why I rebel against a one-size-fits-all approach, one way or the highway; pedagogical principles as gospel; vocal terminology that has no truth in nature or science; that you have to sound a certain way to be successful. I rebel against all of it. I don't want you to sound like someone else. I don't want you to think you have to "sing in a certain voice." I don't want you to hold and hesitate and apologize.

You have ONE voice. That voice can have many facets, many colors, many textures. It is a kaleidoscope of possibilities.

The authenticity of that voice is developed by how you access it and integrate it physically, in order to release it fully. Access and integration of that voice mirror and reflect authenticity and integrity on a physical level.

That voice you are introducing to your physicality, has the ability to discover its own power, balance of resonance, range, colors, timbres, and athleticism. All of that is part of who you are. "Right or wrong" does not come into play. It simply is. And before you or someone you know gets their panties in a twist, we know that sometimes, someone does it all "wrong" pedagogically, and it works.

As you release the language that no longer serves you, you will begin to give yourself permission to become more conscious of what you do, what your possibilities are, and
where they could take you. You are able to consciously discover the language that will serve you moving forward.

If you have something to reveal or a story to tell, if you have something to say that is a truth in your life as a human being, an actor, a speaker, a singer, then your truth can only inhabit the authenticity of your voice. It doesn't belong anywhere else, nor does it belong to anyone else. This is the crucial turning point.

Creating that authenticity does require knowledge and awareness. However, that knowledge needs to be translated into your body and your psyche in order for it to be inhabited with authenticity. We all know what it feels like physically to wear something that doesn't really fit. We can fake comfort on the outside, but we can't wait to change and never have to wear it again! If the authentic voice is truly in development and belongs to you, it should fit as if it was made for you— because guess what, it was! You shouldn't feel like you are faking it.

There is nothing less authentic than "fake it til you make it". Yes, I said it.

If the voice you reveal is truly YOU, then whatever you have to say will be heard and acknowledged. It cannot be easily dismissed.

Is it complex? Yes. Is it work? Yes. Is it an ongoing process? Yes.

Is it worth it? OH, HELL YES. Every single time.

And guess what? You don't have to have it all figured out. You just have to acknowledge that it's possible. Knowledge is power. Your knowledge of your power and your authenticity is your birthright.

Claim it. Begin to claim it. Dare to claim it, or at least dip a toe in the water to see how it feels. See what it reveals, what it brings up and where it leads.

Find your people. Those humans who will help you find it, reveal it, develop it, and encourage you to inhabit it without hesitation or apology, one step at a time.

REFLECTIONS

What motivates you to sing?

What stops you from singing? From auditioning? From sending a submission?

In a perfect world, what is the ideal environment for you to sing in? Dream a little!

What are some practical steps you can take to create that ideal environment right now? In 6 months? In a year?

Beyond, but...

Technique is noticed most markedly in the case of those who have not mastered it.
    - Leon Trotsky

Technique? Sexy?

I told you this isn't a book about technique, and it's not. There are many pedagogical resources you can delve into if you want to learn more science, more physicality, more acoustics, more stuff.

However, let's be clear: good technique is sexy.

When I talk about technical behavior in the studio, I describe technique as "the underwear for the voice." And you should never skimp on underwear. (Those of you who choose to go commando, that's a choice too!) While your vocal underwear must be practical, durable, and reliable, it doesn't have to be granny panties! It must be sexy! It must make you feel fabulous! It should enhance and not detract. If we create technical behavior that is effective, shaped, sculpted, and accessible, it will be there to reveal you, not hide you.

Technique, and the physical behavior of said technique, allows you to discover access into the function and the building of the actual voice. Creating functional behavior allows you to see and observe how your voice responds authentically - in its underwear - without informing it with style or genre.

This is the time to get curious and stay curious about how to build this technical behavior in your body because technique is the foundation to all great singing, no matter the genre or style!

Just as there are foundational garments in the underwear world, so there are in the technical world of voice!

Stay in charge of the process as you continue to explore how that voice feels & how it responds. Learning HOW you process is key: are you a visual learner, an auditory learner, a kinesthetic learner? A little of all? You are now paying attention to that voice, and that physicality that it resides in, instead of just going through the motions of an exercise or a phrase and hoping it works.

The repertoire, style, genre, audition material, or role, are the "outfits and accessories" that wrap around your technique. Without that foundation, nothing will fit right. Don't make me come at you with a Sondheim lyric: "Sometimes when the wrappings fall, there's nothing underneath at all..."

Don't get caught without your underwear. Build your technical behavior from the inside out. Layer it, shape it, reveal it.

Does that mean you have to have it all figured out before you start trying things on and seeing what fits?

Of course not!

You do need to know your voice well enough to know what you need and when you need it. If you don't, you need to find someone who you can trust to help you develop that knowledge. Sometimes it's building, sometimes it's re-assessing, sometimes it's endurance, sometimes it's detailed sculpting, sometimes it's maintenance, sometimes it's health... Sometimes you know these things on your own, and sometimes you need to access them with a second set of ears and eyes. Often, it's a combination of both.

Where you are, what you are doing, and what you are ready to do indicates what you need. Stay present enough to figure out what that is and begin to claim it. Think both athletically and artistically; they go together beautifully. The technical behavior of athleticism and the technical behavior of artistry feed off of each other and nurture each other. What is then created, is the magic of you.

And you know what is really sexy? When the technical behavior of your voice meets your acting intelligence and your understanding of style & genre. How your voice can be revealed in and through language, tone, and nuance without you even being conscious of it, is because of technical behavior.

How you are able to tell that story because of what you have developed, not in spite of what you haven't yet figured out yet, is technical behavior.

You aren't a human hanger showing off the repertoire. You are a unique, authentic singer within the repertoire. We want to see YOU, the character you are inhabiting, and the story you are telling. Only then can your artistry fully and authentically find a place to reside.

    Claim it. Find the places and spaces and professionals you can trust to help facilitate your discovery! Explore it. Then explore it some more.

REFLECTIONS

What is your process for learning? Do you see it? Hear it? Feel it? Speak it? Write it? Visual? Aural? Kinesthetic? Write/Speak? A little of more than one?

Where do you see these processes show up in your technical behavior?

What does your physical technical behavior allow you to do right now?

What would you like that technical behavior to allow you to do in 6 months?

In a year?

What would that take to get there?

Commitment

"The commitment to a practice opens the door to finding a more useful technique." - Seth Godin

Commitment.

The word evokes an awareness, a presence, a questioning, a curiosity, determination, clarity, and follow-through. It can also evoke a clenching of the solar plexus and the jaw, and a fear, and self-doubt. Let's be honest: if we commit, what if it doesn't work???

Yet, if we do NOT commit, how will we ever know? There must be a commitment to the practice, and a commitment to the process of that practice.

So, what is the practice? Literal, in the studio at the piano, working out the technical demands of a piece of music? Working on the technical behavior of the voice itself and harnessing its physicality so you can work on that music?

Or is it the practice of mindset and mental focus in order to create honesty, and then a schedule and structure to explore and discover what is needed from you?

Commitment in practice, whatever that means to you, creates behavior. These behaviors then allow for technical behavior.

What does technical behavior mean to you? Is it the study of pure technique on your own or with a teacher? Is it the further application of said technique to the repertoire you choose to sing? Is it a functional trust of the body - both intrinsic and extrinsic - to "house" the voice effectively? Is it the awareness in isolation in order to integrate into the many layers of artistry to truly carry the artistic result? Or is it something else?

Your commitment to your practice illuminates your authenticity from WITHIN that developed behavior.

Whew. It's a lot, isn't it?

Commitment to your artistry and to your practice can feel very solitary. I suppose it has to be, if we truly understand the uniqueness and individuality of it all.

However, the solitary feeling doesn't mean you are alone. None of us do this alone, or at least we shouldn't. We all need another set of eyes and ears, a different angle of expertise, a collaboration, to help us discover that which we have yet to learn and claim.

A practice is simply this: rehearsing a behavior repeatedly in order to master it and make it yours.

However, what that commitment LOOKS like, how you structure it, and why you approach it in a certain way is up to you. You hold the keys. You have the tools. Yes, you.

So, how do you make that commitment?

Well, start by realizing that you're not in this alone, even in the solitary discovery of practicing the practice! Your teacher, your coach, and your inner circle of advisors are all a part of that commitment.

You and your team must work together to discover what you need and how you will develop it. Taking lessons isn't about me (or any other teacher or coach) telling you what to do. I always tell my clientele that the work to create technical behavior is a collaborative event.

So, ask the questions. Ask all the questions. Listen for suggestions, listen for answers. Take a moment to try. Take a moment to laugh at yourself, and still take your process seriously. The number of times a singer and I have laughed in the studio together must be in the millions. It is truly a cathartic experience. Laughter allows us to stretch and shake it out and enjoy the absurdity of it all. I mean, if we can't laugh, why bother?

Only when the two of us coming together—singer and teacher—can we discover what you are here to do. Together, we will uncover how to access what you are able to do and challenge you to discover what you are not able to do yet, in order to allow the technical development to have a place to reside when the physicality is ready, and the psyche is able.

The process of technical behavior always begins with a question that is then put into physical action.

These questions will break down into more and more detail, and more and more specificity to create a personalized and physicalized technical behavior that only YOU can embody.

Healthy, authentic collaboration allows you to take back into your solitude a sense of being and a sense of doing, knowing that you are not alone in the exploration; Nor are you being judged as you explore. Technical behavior, the actual physical behavior of how you are building the skill and finesse of your vocal technique, requires your consistent commitment—to the process, to the practice, to the time, to the growth, to the frustrating moments that help you discover more efficiency, sustainability, and endurance, and to the exhilarating moments of "ah-ha!" Most of all, it requires commitment to yourself.

Commitment isn't always comfortable, but it's real. You know it is. You know it's real because you see and sense progress. You know it when you are able to tap into more of what is possible because it leads to more ability. Commitment leads to more reliable physical and vocal behavior you can count on to access what it is you want to do. It can also reveal things you never knew you had the potential to do! It leads to knowledge and visceral understanding. It uncovers true confidence.

So, how's your gut? How do you feel reading this?

Really think about it. Are you feeling resistance? Excitement? Maybe dread? All feelings are legitimate. All of them. Don't dismiss a single one. None of them are right or wrong. There is no value judgment in the feeling.

Getting started is easy. Just commit to beginning where you are. Don't go beyond what is right now.

Commit to uncovering the possibility. Commit to discovering the beginning of your process today.

Right now. This week.
One step at a time.

Reflections

What does commitment to technical behavior look like to you? What do you need for this commitment to occur? Why?

What can you put into place to create this reality today? In 6 months? In a year?

Lost in Translation

"Art is craft, not inspiration.[1]" - Stephen Sondheim

The study of voice, the teaching of voice, is both mysterious and miraculous.

Working with intangibles - breath and vibration - and discovering the physicality of where that resides and intensifies is rather remarkable. We often don't think about this clearly, but when we do, it adds to the uniqueness of what we do.

We work with breath we can't see, vibration we can't see, and intrinsic muscles we can't see. We must create a way to create tangibility with the intangible.

Discovering HOW you learn will help you weave together these intangibles.

You might need an anatomy book, a yoga class, a Pilates class, a breath or somatic class, or another type of body work class to help integrate the tangible with the intangible more effectively. Add in the psychology of an artist, which varies widely from human to human, and you have an amazing and messy prospect and project!

And while I love messy, I sometimes wonder how much is lost in translation.

We use many words and phrases to help us understand the voice - from all corners of the process: the singer, the teacher, the coach, the casting table, the conductor, the director.

"Open throat," "breathe from the diaphragm," "in the mask." But do we actually know what those words mean? Whether you are a teacher, a coach, or a singer, how you translate for yourself and for others is crucial to your success and the success of those around you.

---

1. https://www.azquotes.com/quote/789620

Not only do teachers and coaches need to learn how an individual singer learns in order to translate, but so does the singer her/him/themselves.

One of my biggest "ah-ha!" moments as a singer was the realization that I was translating what I heard in the studio literally.

I thought "placement" meant to literally put my voice somewhere physically. I thought "forward" was in front of my face. I tried to literally "place it in the mask". I tried to literally "breathe low," (e-hem, no lungs down there) and literally tried to "get my voice to the back of the house."

All of these things are physically impossible, but I tried. I tried because that's what the words said.

Oh, how I wasted time and energy, only to end up tying myself up in knots - physically and emotionally!

I honestly believe this is a huge missing piece for many singers.

It is crucial to learn how we learn. Only then can we begin to actually understand and embody what is being asked of us.

I am the queen of "why." I always want to know "why." Not to be a pain in the ass (and trust me, I've been accused of being difficult more than a time or two for simply asking why), but because I truly want to understand! I want to understand what you mean when you say XYZ.

I want to understand what that "end result" really means in my body, my breath, my vibration. I want to understand the behavior of breath and support and vibration and acoustic and resonance, and to figure out how that balances my physicality.

This understanding allows me to find out what it means to each individual singer, in order to lather, rinse, and repeat the behavior so it can be easily integrated into their technique.

This allows for the authenticity of the voice, the expression, and the storytelling to be "front and center" at all times. (see what I did there?)

We don't all learn the same way. We don't all process the same way. We don't all have the same psychology, nor the same physiology.

So why would we all experience healthy singing in the same way?

Guess what? It's okay to translate technique. TRANSLATE into your understanding, in order for you to figure out how to do what you need to do and how you do it!

We all hear the same language from many different corners. It's okay to hear the words, then allow them to move through your translation code and to do that.

So how do we get there? What does that take?

Preparation. Understanding. A willingness to discover and uncover. A desire to explore.

An unapologetically curious approach that gives you the momentum to find the answers and creates behaviors that are uniquely and authentically YOU. When we take the time to prepare, to discover and explore, we can eventually translate effectively in the moment.

It's okay if someone uses a word or phrase that isn't what you are actually doing.

Let them call the technique what they want. You need to know the difference and the specificity of how it translates into your body, because guess what? You are the one being asked to do it!

As an exercise, make a list of "singer words." See if you can actually verbalize to yourself what each means. If you can't, that word isn't serving you. Translate it into something you can access, and then do it. It is in the doing that you create the possibility of behavior. Then describe the behavior of that word, or if you have translated it, the word or phrase that you have translated it into, in order for you to inhabit the behavior it represents.

Technical behavior allows for you to reveal what is beyond words. This is the craft.

This is, in my world as a singer, actor & teacher, what I am committed to discover.

REFLECTIONS

Create an ongoing list of "singer words" that we often hear and write down what they mean to you now. If you can't translate it, it isn't serving you, so create another word or phrase to replace it in your lexicon! Here are a few to get you started:

"Low breath" "Forward" "Placement" "Breathe from your diaphragm."

"Put it in the mask."

Keep building on this list and your translations!

A Winding Path

Our journey in the performance industry is not a straight shot, but it pretends to be. It certainly can be sold that way, which creates confusion, doesn't it? We are not doctors, lawyers, accountants, or other professions that have a practical movement of "when this happens, then that happens." We don't get the luxury of graduating from college or conservatory and immediately getting hired for a job, which leads to yet another job.

When we inhabit a "linear process", something like audition, callback, callback, callback (!!), rehearsals, production, we can get side-tracked, confused, and frustrated when that so-called linear process gets broken. When the audition doesn't happen, then what? When there is silence after a callback, then what? When you get through the final callbacks and hear crickets, then what? When you sit in the hallway of an open call all day and never get seen in the room, now what?

What we really need to remind ourselves of is that our true journey remains non-linear. "Journey" often implies a straight line, but as artists and performers, our journey is created as we go, as we stop, as we ponder, and often that does not have a clear destination. Our personal journey is as unique as our fingerprints, and so only we can carve the path we travel on. This can be both frustrating and exhilarating.

When the frustration wants to take over, how can you make room for yourself? Instead of letting outside forces and voices determine your path, what can you do to discover what that journey means to you?

You owe NO ONE an explanation. There's freedom in that. Those that ask linear questions simply do not understand the process. Theirs is not an artistic journey. They are on their own path, and will have to figure it out, just as you are figuring out yours.

You are precisely where you need to be. Keep discovering what that means, and the journey will continue to reveal itself.

QUESTIONS TO REFLECT ON

What did you expect would happen when you chose this journey?

How would you describe where you are right now on this journey?

What do you know about this journey that you didn't know at the beginning?

What would you like to do next?

What do you need to put into place and act upon to make that a possibility?

The Psyche & Mindset
The Choosing

"I chose and my world was shaken, so what?
The choice may have been mistaken, the choosing was not."
- **Stephen Sondheim, Sunday in the Park with George**

Let's just agree that the business - no matter what area of the business you are pursuing - is not fair. It needs change, and a whole lot more. So, let's take it out of the equation for a moment.

What can you, the artist, control?

You can control the pursuit. The pursuit of developing your talent, your craft, and most importantly, your mindset, is all within your control.

Mindset is the driving force for your talent, guiding how you move into your career - at whatever level or location.

Mindset gives you permission to create and develop craft, allowing you to see your patterns and to acknowledge your emotional and psychological intelligence. It gives permission to change what needs changing in order to access what you need.

Mindset affects attitude, self-talk, and motivation.

For some, it can also induce self-sabotage and crippling self-doubt. However, it can also give you freedom to explore, to release, to learn and to behave and respond in a way that is healthy, open, and available.

I have seen just as many "unprofessional" mindsets trying to pursue a career than I have seen "professional" mindsets in community theater.

Mindset is EVERYTHING, no matter where you are.

So, what is the magic here? Choice.

And what can sabotage a professional mindset? Excuses.

You can choose to be professional with your attitude. You can choose to pursue excellence and craft. You can choose to develop your talent. You can choose your behavior. You can choose how you speak to yourself. You can choose to acknowledge how the business is a pain in the ass and choose to do your work anyway. You can choose to stand up, to call out, to stand firm, and create boundaries.

You can also choose to walk away if you aren't feeling it, if you aren't aligned with it, or if you don't want it anymore. You can choose to move in another direction.

You may not feel like you have many choices, but you do. And there is great empowerment in choice.

You can also choose to make excuses.

Mindset can create momentum, or it can completely debilitate you. One is a professional mindset; one is not.

Is it that easy? Yes, it kind of is.

Sometimes the choice won't feel natural right away. Sometimes you won't "feel" it. Sometimes you will know, and sometimes you'll just have to go with the choice and see where it leads. It's just the beginning, but it's crucial.

Is it overwhelming? Only if you choose to do it all at once!

If you are wanting to overhaul your mindset, work with it a step at a time.

Start with simply becoming aware of the pitfalls you may have set up for yourself and work one at a time.

Are you aware of what you need? How about what you do not need, or what is standing in your way that you have created?

With self-sabotage, it's very human to blame outside forces first. No value judgment - we've all done it! It doesn't need to be anybody's fault, including yours. It's just about acknowledging that there's a roadblock that needs to be moved, and then figuring out how to move it!

You have choices. About everything.

You are never a failure if you choose, Why? Because if that choice doesn't make sense, then you simply make another choice!

Doubt, dry spells, a time of walking through the desert, are all part of the artist's journey as they pursue their career choice, and quite honestly, a life choice.

Are you willing to find the mindset to navigate that? What are you willing to do to stay the course? To change the course? To be the change? To be the course?

Begin.

It's not simple, and yet, it is.

Just begin.

The beginning is simply wherever you are right now. Discover what you have, where you are, and what you need to do to begin.

Seek the mindset you wish to have, and let that mindset lead, walking alongside your talent and the craft you are developing and are striving to reveal.

Your mindset can create a place for you; a place that is unique to you and what you have to offer, what you can do, and what you can say.

The mindset creates the living space for authenticity to thrive.

If you want change, be the change!

Choose a beginning. If you have to, do it daily. Simply choose. Then make another choice. And another. You have this magic within you, even when it feels overwhelming.

Choose the magic, instead of the overwhelm and see what happens!

REFLECTIONS

Do you currently have a scarcity mindset or an abundance mindset? What determines that for you?

Make a list of places either mindset or both manifests itself; is there rigidity? Is there fight or flight? Is there acceptance? Grace?

When you feel overwhelmed, how does it manifest itself?

When you are content, what does that look like?

If you could choose ANYTHING right now for your life, your artistry, your career, what would it be?

What would you choose or need to RELEASE to gain that?

What small mindset choice can you make each day to begin to shift? Journaling? Gratitude? Mantra?

Process or Product Mindset

As I continue my teaching journey, I have discovered that artists and performers are drawn to two different aspects of performance: the process and the end result.

Those who are drawn to the process, love the study, the development, the discovery. They are committed to craft and to diving deep into themselves, even as they dive even more deeply into the material. They could be happy simply studying, going to classes, and discovering new ways of exploring craft. They don't dismiss the finished product but would prefer to stay in the rehearsal room with the tape on the floor. That is where the magic happens for them. The stage is a byproduct, not the finish line.

Some are drawn to the stage. They love the finished result. They are drawn to the audition room and the dazzle of footlights, the costumes, the audience, and all that the theater evokes in their minds. This is where they want to be. This is where the magic happens for them.

After many years of teaching and observing many different people, I know these traits reveal themselves fairly quickly. There is not a right or wrong in these traits. It simply reveals where an artist's psychology is coming from and how that leads them.

The result can inform the process and the process can inform the result. If we want to be truly realized performing artists, or performers with craft or discipline, we must allow both to inform us fully.

Someone who says they want to be onstage but will not commit to the study of the craft to find the stage, may have a certain amount of "success," depending on their natural ability, timing, and luck. However, "the stage and only the stage" will not sustain fully.

"Patchwork craft" does not sustain talent. It does not build upon a talent, nor does it serve that talent. Frankly, it doesn't serve the stage either.

To be on stage means you have something to say. To say it, there must be someone to hear it. That audience deserves the real craft, the authentic performer, the true storyteller.

True technique is never seen once the footlights come up. That work is done behind the scenes to give the illusion of none.

This is the real magic. This is also really hard work.

However, if it's work you commit to, it's not exhausting, is it?

Lack of technique begins to show ragged over time and the lights are not forgiving.

Ever.

Someone who loves the process can sometimes get lost in its perceived safety and never quite find what is needed to play once they're in the audition room. Process can take on a "by rote" formula at times: regular lessons, regular classes, rinse, and repeat. It is safe because it is predictable. It can create a false sense of safety because it isn't always required to move past the routine. The result of the process begins to wear thin.

When process becomes a loop that you can sleepwalk through, is it process anymore, or has it become mindless busy work?

When we observe ourselves to see what we are doing, what would happen if we saw what isn't there to keep the momentum moving fully?

Those who crave the process can continue to build the momentum to include a follow-through of discovery in the audition room, in order to be seen and heard and then have an opportunity to take that craft to another level of discovery, and ultimately, creation on stage.

The process gives you permission to step into the room when the door presents itself, instead of hesitating and saying, "I'm not ready yet."

If you claim the process fully and honestly, you will be ready. You will be ready for the door you choose or the door that chooses you. The choosing is key.

Those who crave the footlights can continue to see that as their goal but must also allow for what must be developed to get there. Simple desire is not enough. What about channeling all that energy and dreaming into a regular course of study to reveal to yourself what is possible when you get that opportunity? What about learning how to sustain that craft once you are invited in to play? This is crucial for you.

So, trust where your initial momentum takes you. Process or product? Then give yourself permission to find out how to weave one toward the other, as you claim more authenticity in both. Let the two interweave fully in your personal process of craft and product.

We are never done. We are never finished. This is a wonderful thing. It gives you permission to observe, change direction, stay present, stay curious. It allows you to follow that spark that caught your eye, and to move you in a direction you might not have considered before. This is life. This is art. This is being.

Sit back and observe, then decide what you will pick up and how you want to proceed. The door does appear. If it hasn't yet, it might be time to make a decision on what you pick up next. YOU choose.

Let the door appear.

REFLECTIONS

Where are you currently, in process or product mindset?

Why is that particular mindset important to you?

Do you feel resistance or acceptance/acknowledgement of the other mindset? where does it manifest itself?

If resistance, what 3 steps can you take to release that resistance a bit?

If acceptance, what 3 steps can you take to integrate the mindsets for yourself?

Longevity

What does longevity even mean? How do we define it for ourselves?

The life span, the shelf life, the duration, the viability, the relevance?

Is there endurance? Is there knowledge?

We live in a feast or famine business as artists in the industry, so it needs to be a subterranean longevity that prepares us for those seemingly meager times. Those are often the times that make us question why we are doing this at all. You know the ones.

I see the extremes of this regularly in the studio. I see the singer who somehow hopes for a quick fix in order to have enough to walk into a room, knock out a fabulous audition and hope it sticks.

My question is always: What if you get the job? What if you can "suck in" long enough so the seams don't bust, for them to hire you? What happens when you relax and don't hold your breath?

The quick fix never works for longevity. Never. If you are able to make an adjustment in the studio, it isn't "fixed." It just shows you that you are able to now begin to discover what could become a behavior if you commit to it. It's the first step.

What you perceive as a "quick fix" is an illusion. It might be bright and shiny for a minute, but don't let it fool you. Don't allow it to create another voice in your head that takes you down that path of, "Oh, I got this!" The only one falling for it, at the end of the day, is you.

What about being in it for the long haul? It doesn't have to mean slogging and fatigue, and depression and disillusionment! It can mean commitment to each moment, to a lifestyle, a behavior, a schedule. It really means commitment to yourself.

YOU are the long haul. You aren't a quick fix. You are your own longevity, your own sustainability. You and only you can commit to that. This kind of commitment keeps you focused through the times of famine, the dips, the slow times. The times when you are ready to gnaw off your arm. Your long haul will not take your focus away. Your long haul will simply give you permission to sit down and rest, and then get up and keep working, keep discovering, keep growing when it is time. And you know what? You are worth every moment of it.

It's easy to get side-tracked with a quick fix because it catches your eye and doesn't require much. That's the point: it isn't much. It may or may not be helpful, and it is like a flash in the pan. When it's done, it's done, and you won't find it again. There is no depth to it, no grounding, no anchor. Flash and gone.

Watching people chase the quick fix is very hard to observe, but we are each responsible for our own path and our own ability to see and discover, to reveal and absorb.

The long haul requires fortitude. It requires a commitment that reveals the integrity of the human being and artistic spirit that rises to its occasion. It commands attention and demands your complete and utter dedication. It is deep, and high, and full, and anchored. It gives you freedom to play, to explore, to create. It is not heavy. The long haul is buoyant and pliable.

Longevity is creation. It is artistic depth. Longevity is anchored in truth and authenticity.

Acknowledge the lure of the quick fix, the flash pot, the jazz hands. Just don't fall for it.

Walk on by and pick up the tools, learn the language, and discover the authenticity of your longevity.

The long haul doesn't need to be heavy. It just needs to be YOURS.

REFLECTIONS

> What does longevity mean to you, in your development?
> How can you nurture this longevity development in yourself?

Who do you admire that exemplifies this type of longevity? What do you observe about them that reveals this longevity?

The Power of Language

I continue to learn and experience the power of language as I remain a student of behavior and mindset. I don't mean just learning to speak, or write, or comprehend, but the power of language on the psyche of self.

What language do you use with yourself? What is your self-talk? How do you treat yourself through language? Are you consciously aware of how you speak to yourself? What are your patterns? What are your loops? What are your cycles?

Are you even consciously aware of any of this? If not, guess what? It's time.

We are often so focused on what we need to do next, what we need to do better, what we aren't doing enough of... And, in all that language, our self-talk may be the most defeating of all.

Guess what?

We have control over our language.

Toni Morrison says it most eloquently: "Oppressive language does more than represent violence; it is violence; does more than represent the limits of knowledge; it limits knowledge."

You have a choice. You can decide how you speak. What you speak. When you speak. Why you speak. The language you use is crucial to your mindset, mental and psychological health, spiritual well-being, and artistic health and nurturing.

Your language has the potential to be your success.

Your language has the potential to be your demise.

Speak to yourself with care, with love, attention, compassion, passion, with intention, with gratitude.

Speak to create, not to destroy. Speak to motivate, not isolate. Speak truth, not obstruction. Speak to possibility, not powerlessness.

Use the language with yourself that you would use with your best friend. Use it with authority, use it with energy, use it with authenticity.

You are enough. You are more than enough. You are a living, breathing human being with possibility, potential, and purpose.

Create the language you need to develop momentum. Give yourself permission to be where you are, to live your life and your journey authentically and individually as you are. AS. YOU. ARE.

If you even start with "yeah, but" I am going to lodge one of my many, many stilettos in the middle of your forehead. Trust me, I have enough (I have to do it to myself from time to time too)!

Yeah, but.... Yeah, but what? Yeah, but you aren't enough? Why? Says who? Yeah, but you shouldn't? Really? Yeah, but all the things? All the things. What are those things to you? What do they matter to your journey? Where do they belong? Where do YOU belong?

Release the self-talk that does not serve you, one statement at a time. Quit apologizing for being precisely where you are. Stop being potential, and begin to claim the being of you, the beginning of YOU.

Too much?

No. You are never too much.

Be who you are, how you are, where you are.

Be your language. Be the language you use with yourself.

I will share with you a very, very personal anecdote with you here. A number of years ago, I was ranting about myself to my husband. He let me finish, and then said, very quietly and poignantly: "You realize that if I beat on you the way you just beat on yourself through language, I would be in jail."

There it was. My "a-ha" moment. My pivotal moment. My clarity of self-talk and time to pivot, step ball change. (You didn't think I had it all figured out, did you?).

Language is.

You are.

Both are vivid, both have life, consequence, and motivation. Both can be destructive and mutilating, but both can also create and illuminate.

It's another choice. YOUR choice.

Allow yourself the respect, love, patience, and courage to speak authentically. Allow yourself to change the language when it begins to loop into the speech that doesn't serve you. Challenge the self to pursue clarity and definition and not fall for the easy way out.

How to start? Leave sticky notes for yourself on the bathroom mirror, on the fridge, on your binders, at the piano - wherever you find yourself. Simply start with "You are..." fill in that blank.

Try gratitude journaling. List three things you are grateful for in the morning, and three things you are grateful for before bed. There is nothing too small to be grateful for.

What do you need to do? Speak to it. Honor it. Do it.

Action through language begins with you. You have THAT kind of control. It's immense, and it's magnificent.

REFLECTIONS

Get yourself some colorful sticky notes. Write down "I AM... (you fill it in - but they need to be POSITIVE) Do this every day for a week and leave them where you see them every single day!

What are you grateful for in your actual singing?

What are you grateful for in your day-to-day life?

Who are you grateful for in your singing life?

Who are you grateful for in your day to day?

Create a mantra and write it down. Then speak it out loud. Louder. LOUDER (and well-supported, please)!

Reinvention

Can you reinvent yourself and re-emerge?

In a word: absolutely.

So often, we feel we can't stop or take time off. We can't, we can't, we can't for fear we will be lost in the shuffle or forgotten and have to start over.

Wrong.

If we never stop, never take time off, never take a moment to catch our breath, we burn out. Burnout makes us cynical, and we lose the love and the passion for what we do in the first place.

If we believe we are artistic souls and spirits, we need to feed and nurture that passion in order to keep the well full, so we can draw on it and feed our artistic lives.

Come close. I'll share with you this little secret: the business isn't going anywhere.

It will be there if you decide to take a vacation, travel, explore another avenue. It will be there if you decide to have a life outside of theater for a minute or two.

If you are answering "yes, but..." Slow. Your. Roll.

The business isn't going anywhere. If you don't take time to create a life that allows you to breathe, explore, rest, laugh, BE - you aren't going anywhere either. You aren't early, you aren't late, you aren't anywhere.

When things feel or begin to feel stale, mundane, or joyless, it's time to re-invent. That can mean so many different things and can be just as creative as you choose! The possibilities are ENDLESS. They only need to make sense to you. No explanation necessary. No approval needed from outsiders. No permission needed.

If it gets you excited or interests you, focus on it. Explore it. Explore you in it. It doesn't mean you are turning your back on theater or any other pursuit in the arts. It means you are bigger than the hustle, and you are turning yourself toward you.

Embrace that reinvention. Explore where it takes you, knowing that when you choose to return, the business will still be there.

You have chosen yourself, and you will bring more into your artistic world (and how you choose to be seen in auditions, your social media presence, in classes and lessons, in workshops, or with your colleagues and peers) if this re-invention is allowed to be explored and embraced.

How you reinvent yourself is up to you. Let your gut lead you. Let your head acknowledge the reinvention and purpose. Allow yourself to gestate and grow there as long as you need to; you can always return and rediscover THAT as well.

Reinvention allows you control of your narrative. Once you re-emerge and begin exploring the business and how you fit there, often the questions will come: Who are you? Where have you been? How come I haven't seen you before/in a while? Don't let the questions throw you!

Let the curiosity of others allow you permission to have a narrative, and don't be afraid to create a succinct answer that keeps them curious!

"I took some time off to travel/explore/have another life. Now I am back, refreshed and with more to offer!"

"I gave myself permission to explore other interests, knowing the roles I am really wanting to play are still waiting for me to be ready".

You are an artist; you can craft a response that is uniquely and creatively yours!

You have so many possibilities in how you emerge and re-emerge. So many possibilities lie in how you answer the questions that may come your way. Embrace that curiosity, too.

Allow yourself permission to be still and begin to discover how, why, and when. It can happen more than once. Re-invention isn't a one and done!

Your artistic life has no expiration date. It will continue to grow because of how you view the world and how you live your life.

Audition, class, coaching, lesson, lather, rinse, and repeat does not have to be a way of life. That grind gets tired very, very quickly if there is not a desire that motivates you.

Learning how to step away, to step into, to mix it up, to add something, to take something away, to be more discerning, is crucial to your re-invention and your re-emerging! It is a dance that you create as you do it.

Allow the possibility of you to emerge in your time. Know you can create it fully.

Creating isn't starting over, it's just beginning from where you are.

Take a breath and move into it at your own pace. No "yes, but..." but rather, "Yes, AND..."

REFLECTIONS

What do you feel passionate about that IS NOT singing?

What exhausts you about your life right now?

What excites you about your life right now?

If you could sustain 3 things/feelings in your life, what would they be?

If you could do anything else in your life right now, what would you want it to be?

If you could have a full week of self-care, what would you do? Or not do? Where would you go? Or not go?

What are the common "feels" when you are singing well, and when you are feeling passionate about that thing that isn't singing? Is there a common feeling? Are they different?

The Artist

"And suddenly you know: It's time to start something new and trust the magic of beginnings." - Meister Eckhart

"And above all, watch with glittering eyes the whole world around you because the greatest secrets are always hidden in the most unlikely places. Those who don't believe in magic will never find it."
- Roald Dahl

Magic

As I continue to morph and change and journey, I have many more questions than I have answers. As I explore what is now and what is next and make room for that, the idea of magic continues to be a part of my sphere.

What is magic anyway? What does it evoke? How is it created?

The definition is very personal. Perhaps that's the most effective way in: how do you interpret it? How do you recognize it? Is magic something that is instant because you want it so? Is it something you create specifically, or something someone creates for you? Is it wishing, hoping, yearning?

Maybe.

The word "magic" could be a noun or verb. One definition is: move, change, or create by or as if by magic.

It is created through art and skill. Through ability and talent. It is a practice.

Interesting, no?

It isn't "let me wave my wand and blow unicorn glitter on you, and voilà -, you will have what you think you need." No, not at all. What you think you need may not be "it" at all.

Magic is revealed through action. It is created through, created by, created when, created as action.

Magic happens when all the forces are aligned. It isn't perfection, it's alignment. It's energy. It's focused authenticity.

Okay, before you start rolling your eyes at Susan's "woo-woo," let's ponder this further.

What if the journey is not to add more, but to reveal more?

What if the journey is to acknowledge the "imposter syndrome" you often carry in your peripheral, and release it? To see who and what you really are?

What if the journey isn't linear at all, but rather deeper and higher and more expansive all at once?

A singer once commented during a session on something we were working on technically, and said, "So, is this the last piece of the puzzle?"

It took me off guard, in all honesty. I have never viewed technique or craft as done. If it is a linear achievement, then there is no depth nor dimension, nor ability to create in the moment. So, I answered, "No. There is no 'done.' There is only where you are and what you can do with it."

Perhaps that's where the magic happens: when all the points of discovery come together through craft, intellect, intuition, technique, psyche, response, mindset, to uncover the reality of the moment; When the reality of the breath, the word, the phrase, the note, the character is revealed authentically and woven seamlessly.

So quit trying so hard to make it happen (or to stop it from happening). Quit trying to control it all, you dear sweet Type A human that I know so well. Quit trying to convince yourself that it's all or nothing. Quit trying to be perfect.

Explore.

Discover.

Journey not to "become," but to actually "reveal" and "uncover."

You may find in revealing, honing, and committing to the truth, something uniquely yours, uniquely you. It's messy, it's delicious, it's liberating. It's true.

Strive to explore what you do not yet own. And own it. Own the doubts, the fears, the good, the bad and the ugly.

Perhaps that's where the magic begins. That's where I choose to begin. Each and every time.

REFLECTIONS

How do YOU define magic?

What is one magical thing that has happened to you?

Why do you define it as magical?

Have you ever experienced magic in the theater as an audience member? If yes, what was it? What happened?

Have you ever experienced a magical moment on stage? In a lesson or coaching? In a class? What happened? How did it make you feel?

Abracadabra & Audacity

"Abracadabra" comes from the Aramaic phrase avra kehdabra, meaning "I will create as I speak".

"Audacity" can mean a willingness to take bold risks.

Often, audacity is assumed to mean something negative, rude, or disrespectful.

Audacity actually has polar opposites in its definition. It means boldness, grit, daring, fearlessness, bravery, courage.

Perhaps its definition has to do with how another person sees audacity in you.

You define your audacity; it is revealed in your actions. How someone else sees that audacity reveals more about them than it does you.

The audacity and the artist easily go hand in hand - now, more than ever.

We are exploring new territory. If we are to inhabit it, we must be bold, we must be fearless, we must be brave. There is no other choice if we want the change that is necessary.

Being scared or uncertain can co-exist with audacity. Anxiety can be present. "I don't know" is perfectly aligned with "do it anyway."

As artists, we are often a riddle wrapped in an enigma. Our times certainly seem that way, as we observe, release, and forge ahead.

Here's what I know, at least today: Theater, and all things performance and artistic, will re-emerge into more, into new, into next. We are a community that, by nature, morphs and evolves. We must. There is nothing in our history that tells us otherwise. Artists define our times. We breathe life into now, and into the next.

Find your audacity. Claim your abracadabra. Now, more than ever, you can be bold and fearless and firmly stand your ground, without apology or excuse and create as you speak!

We all have work to do. Your audacity directed by your artistry is part of the solution, part of the next, part of the new - just like mine is. We are in this together.

Embrace your warrior grit and let's keep working, trying, revealing. We've got this.

From each of our corners, we continue to shape our society, our humanity, and our times.

Artistic audacity has the power to do just that.

History tells us to keep doing what we do. Be audacious. Feel that kick in the ass from what has come before, and begin to forge into the new, and the next. Release what you can't carry and move forward. Sit down when you are tired. Nap when you need to rest. The reveal will be spectacular when audacity and artist join hands and commit to each other.

That's our superpower. We have had it all along.

Abracadabra!

REFLECTIONS

Our collective superpower is audacity. What is your personal superpower?

How does that superpower manifest in your artistic life?

How would you like that superpower to grow and develop? What would it look like?

Who has a superpower you admire? Why do you admire them?

What can you learn from observing that person and how they use that superpower?

"Water does not resist. Water flows. When you plunge your hand into it, all you feel is caress. Water is not a solid wall, it will not stop you. But water always goes where it wants to go, and nothing in the end can stand against it. Water is patient. Dripping water wears away a stone. Remember that, my child. Remember, you are half water. If you can't go through an obstacle, go around it. Water does." - Margaret Atwood

Artistic Energy

If you are an artist, you are forever one, from the moment you wake up to your last breath. Whether you make a living making your art is a completely separate issue.

So, how do you feed that artistic energy?

Some days, the body, the psyche, the spirit simply does not want to pursue, or practice, or move. Sometimes, we are just tired. From what doesn't even matter.

Is it okay? Of course, it is! We must remain sensitive to allow for our artistic lives to grow, and in being sensitive, we often take in more than we can actually deal with. Ah, the daily conundrum!

On the days you are exhausted, depleted, discouraged, just don't wanna...what do you do?

Giving yourself permission just to be where you are is difficult. Trust me, I know. However, the stillness is crucial to rejuvenating and replenishing what we need to continue to thrive. I am still learning how to do that, too.

We are often encouraged to do something for our business and for our artistry each day. On a perfect day, that works. But some days, we simply need to sit still. We need to experience not doing. We need the space to decompress, both physically and psychologically, so re-entry can occur. This is why we often get sick. Our energy has been over-taxed, and our bodies simply say, "No, no more... You gotta sit down and nurture yourself."

It seems so simple, doesn't it? HA! I know it all too well.

So how can you "not do" and replenish? Do you have the rituals in place to allow for "you" time? If it is your time and your choice and your decision, it will feed your soul, psyche, and artistic life.

Give yourself permission to not practice, to skip that audition, to mark in rehearsal. Allow yourself to not please everyone all of the time (if you are a recovering people-pleaser, as I am, this is a hard one!).

Give yourself permission to spend a little more time sleeping, having another cup of coffee, look at a magazine, watch something mindless on your favorite streaming service, or unfollow those who add stress to your social media feeds!

When we slow down enough to allow ourselves to be transported to that stillness, the energy will reveal itself to us. This is when artistic energy meets artistic temperament and allows for growth.

"I have no energy" should be a red flag. You simply need you for a little while. And guess what? "You" is kinda wonderful and worth it.

The artistic energy of you needs as much care and attention as the technical behavior you are developing in your craft, as the score you are studying or the monologue you are developing. The artistic energy of you needs the focus and realization that you give to working out passaggio, breathing, or resonance as you work the transitions of registers!

So, replenish often, otherwise you are living on fumes. No transformation of any kind can last on that. Transformation needs energy. Your energy.

Permission granted.

REFLECTIONS

Are you aware when you are running out of energy?

How does it manifest? What are the signs?

Do you actually DO something about it, and if so, what?

If you don't, what happens? Is there a pattern?

What 2 boundaries can you put in place right now to give you more space on a daily basis to replenish your artistic energy?

What permissions can you give yourself this week to release from your "to do" list?

What are two things you can say "no" to this week that will help you?

What are two things you can allow yourself to claim to replenish energy this week?

The Essential Artist

You are essential.

YOU. ARE. ESSENTIAL.

Essential is needed & necessary. It is the basic part of living. It is vital.

You, as artist, are all these things.

The paradigm may shift, the location may change, the way of creating may need innovation and exploration, but you? You as artist, are essential. That will never, EVER change.

Creative energy is in motion, even when it's still. Energy is like that. Painters who create "still life" still breathe life into their work. "Capturing" something artistically simply allows it to be held in a container for the observer to take it in. All of these things are in motion. The motion and movement happen because of, and in spite of, everything around us.

I observe and take part in so much creative energy from artists. I have the privilege and honor of sharing their observations, their creations, their journeys, their truths.

The essence of an artist is how that artist lives. It is in how that artist breathes, in how that artist views the world and tells the story that they are called to tell. It is in how that artist vibrates.

The form of that essence changes, morphs, and adapts, but it is always present in the artist.

What form does your essence, your calling, your desire, take? How are you holding space for that? Where is your creativity and your artistic fingerprint showing up and revealing itself? These things make momentum possible.

If your essence/calling is to draw, to paint, to sculpt, to dance, to sing, to play, to write…. Then do that. Don't wait for "a place" to inhabit in order to do it. DO IT. The place reveals itself when the action is taken. That is what is essential.

The "essential" changes the molecules around you.
The change begets more change.
The change challenges the paradigms.
The paradigms shatter if they are not built on anything true.

The artist dares to shine a light on that truth. The truth continues to emerge out of chaos, and the essence of the artist is there to interpret, to elaborate, to simplify, to reach in and pull out the story that needs to be told.

Artists are not extra. We are not frivolous. We are not to be dismissed. We are consistently essential to our society, to our humanity, to our world.

I will say it again: artists define the times we live in. We must. The stories need to be revealed and told - with a bright follow spot - in order for humanity to emerge into its next. If no one is there to capture, to express, to tell the story, then how do we learn? How do we grow? How do we evolve?

Being essential is heavy, and its demand is huge. We, as artists, are pliable and resourceful, creative, and innovative. We can handle tough. However, we need community and self-love to balance. We need to acknowledge our self-worth.

Take a breath. Reach out. Give yourself permission. Do not dismiss your essential-ness.

Embrace the change and mold it into what you can carry.

Sit down when you are tired.

Replenish, reignite, refuel, and recommit to the essential of you. Let that lead you, reveal you. Let that inspire you to take action.

REFLECTIONS

Does saying, "I am essential" make you uncomfortable? Why or why not?

Who is essential in your personal life? And why?

Who is essential in your artistic life? And why?

What makes you essential? (and p.s. Yes, you are!)

What makes you essential to others around you, personally and professionally?

"**May your work be compelling and original. May it be profound, touching, contemplative, and unique.** May it help us to reflect on the question of what it means to be human, and may that reflection be blessed with heart, sincerity, candor, and grace. May you overcome adversity, censorship, poverty and nihilism, as many of you will most certainly be obliged to do. May you be blessed with the talent and rigor to teach us about the beating of the human heart in all its complexity, and the humility and curiosity to make it your life's work. And may the best of you - for it will only be the best of you, and even then only in the rarest and briefest moments - succeed in framing that most basic of questions, "how do we live?" Godspeed." – John Malkovich

Remaining Unapologetic

AM I DOING TOO MUCH? AM I NOT DOING ENOUGH?

Stop. Take a breath. Release it.

What about changing the focus of "doing" right now? Action is happening, and action will happen. Soon, we will be called to be fully in action in our creative lives.

What about being unapologetically artistic and seeing what happens?

What does this mean? You decide.

It could mean simply to release the need to make excuses for the doing or the non-doing.

It could mean embracing your creativity quietly, personally, gently, and tenderly.

It could mean embracing it loudly, publicly, without backing down.

It could mean both.

Being unapologetically artistic allows you permission to be with your inner Muse and follow the lead.

It allows your creativity to show up in different ways.

It allows you to create boundaries.

It allows you to still say "no" during a pandemic, or at any other time.

It allows you to learn to be more pliable.

It allows you permission to rest. To recover. To simply be still.

It allows you permission to move. To test the energy and be energized.

The artistic energy of you can find solace and space in the smallest of things just as effectively as in a larger project.

It gives permission to hope. To be less judgmental of self. To compare less. To fuss less.

It gives permission to care. To rage. To cry. To get excited. To feel blue. To understand. To question.

It gives permission to simply hold space. It becomes and probably has always been the container we've been too busy to recognize has always been there to hold our artistic energy fully.

Be unapologetically artistic. Recognize the absolute unique presence you carry with you through the day. Don't make excuses. Don't shrink away from it or dismiss it.

Be simply unapologetic. Simply artistic. Be aware, pliable, accountable, flexible, curious, creative, inclusive, excited. Never all or nothing.

Always being. Crucially being.

Breathe some life into that space, and don't apologize for that, either.

REFLECTIONS

How are you being unapologetically artistic today?

As you look at the week ahead, what are you giving yourself permission to do? To feel? To allow?

As you look at the week ahead, where can your unapologetic artistry show up?

How can you remain unapologetic yet open to collaborate with others?

The Craft

"Fall in love with the masterpiece, and also the paint on the floor." - Morgan Harper Nichols

Get Ready, Be Ready, Stay Ready

The artistic process never stops.

It can lay dormant, building up momentum. It can change direction and take on different forms. It can re-focus, re-generate, re-boot. It is always there.

The artistic process stays ready, or at least stays accessible.

It then becomes a decision and choice to throw the covers off and engage, or not.

Are you ready? Is it time to get ready and stay ready?

There is no value judgment if you have gone dormant. Your artistic energy has been waiting to revive and begin to pick up steam.

Start wherever you are. No 'what ifs', no woulda-coulda-shoulda. Just now. Just you.

Baby steps. Shake the cobwebs out. Start stretching again. Start plotting out your daily course again. Start exploring what your artistic craft needs, what it doesn't, what is old, what could be new.

Begin with what you know. Begin with what you are able to do now. Let that build the momentum again!

There is nothing worse than not being ready when the opportunity reveals itself.

Don't hesitate. Just start exploring to see where you are and begin to move toward the readiness of where you want to be.

No comparison. No judgment. No second guessing.

This is a fresh start in a famished world.

We need art more than ever.

You are part of that.

We need the stories, the inspiration, the tears, the laughter, the community of sharing and experiencing together, and of healing together.

Being ready to experience the stories—and to tell the stories —is part of the craft.

Get ready. Stay ready. BE ready.

REFLECTIONS

What does "being ready" mean to you?

What 3 things you can do every day to get ready to inhabit your craft?

What 3 things can you do every day to be ready with your craft right now?

What 3 things can you do to stay ready with your craft?

Practicing Craft

"Craft is the visible edge of art." — David Bayles

What does "practicing your craft" mean?

I suppose it can mean different things to different people. I would like to challenge the language and allow permission to claim the phrase fully.

You don't need to wait to practice. You don't need an audience to practice. If you are an artist, your craft is in continual metamorphosis and transformation. It might be realized on stage, on set, and with an audience, but you work out the details—often in solitude—in order to be ready for that particular point.

Language reveals. What language do you speak to yourself? What language do you speak out loud? It's worth the observation in order to truly find out where you are and how you are engaging.

As an artist, our craft is influenced from beyond the stage. It is influenced from beyond the specificity of our realized vocation, and our realized craft. Craft is the way in.

What do you do when you aren't practicing, as it relates to your specific artistic pursuit? How is that practice of action, observation, integration influencing what you do when you stretch the voice? Begin to embody a song or aria? A monologue? Pick up a paint brush? Put on your pointe shoes?

Practice has so much subterranean depth that is never seen by anybody, but fully informs what you, the artist, does. It's never seen, but it's subliminally felt. That practice needs nurturing from all directions!

If you think you aren't practicing your craft, figure out what practice means. Figure out what that craft actually is. What is informing your choices? What are you choosing to believe? What are you choosing to dismiss? Why?

If you feel like you need an audience to perform, why? What does that do for the craft? Is it your craft that needs an audience? Or does it need you first?

There are no right or wrong answers here. Just the exploration. Just the discovery. The revealing. The exposing.

Some of these realizations are subtle. Some are not.

Some of us revel in the practice and the practicING and exploration, others of us crave the discovery in the rehearsal. Some embrace the audience and a fully realized production. Some of us find the journey in all three.

Perhaps, right now, you aren't "practicing" in what might be seen as a traditional way. You aren't vocalizing, you aren't stretching, you aren't accessing the physicality of your instrument to make a place for your craft to reside.

Perhaps, right now, your artistic energy is being channeled into something else that is more subliminal. If you are an artistic spirit, there's a very good chance that's happening, even if you are unaware. Commit to that awareness. You might shock yourself by what it reveals!

All of that artistic energy infuses and influences your craft. It doesn't go away. It simply integrates into how your craft will respond over time. Latent or realized, that energy doesn't disappear. EVER.

Perhaps, by staying present and observing the details of what you might be taking for granted, it will give you a fuller picture of where you are right now.

You the artist, you the human being, you the craftsperson, are practiced. To practice is action. Action is in motion. Motion can build momentum. Momentum can inspire. Inspiration can reach deeply in the soul of the artist to reveal more possibility. Possibility can create. Creation needs craft. It becomes a full circle moment.

And so, there is permission to observe, to realize, to dig deep, to challenge, to be still and to settle in as you practice craft through so many facets of you. You do know that there are many facets of you, right? And each facet is required.

May it create for you another discipline moving into the next, where it can be realized. Just don't dismiss this magical time of possibility within your own transformation.

Practicing craft may have linear aspirations, but it has timeless possibility in every breath and each "ah-ha" moment.

Practice the possibility. Lean in and observe. Let the observation fuel the passion of why you are there in the first place.

REFLECTIONS

Are you "practicing" traditionally? What does that look like?
Are you "practicing" subliminally? What does that look like?
How will you intentionally commit to practice this week?
How will you intentionally inhabit craft this week?
How are they the same/different for you?

The Secret of Craft

"Creativity takes courage." – Henri Matisse

As artists, we hold many secrets within us.
The Nikola Tesla quote goes like this:

"If you want to find the secrets of the Universe, think in terms of Energy, Frequency, and Vibration."

I love this. As singers, this is where we live. This is where we thrive! This is how we weave the uniqueness of our voice together. What we utilize in language and storytelling is woven into the voice and becomes a part of these secrets that lives in the space between.

The intimacy of these secrets is part of your storytelling. The creative process and the craft develop tangible results while living in these secret spaces.

As artists, we embody these secrets, sometimes without even realizing how powerful they truly are.

This is the responsibility we have, and the challenge we are given, should we decide to accept it.

Go gently. Acquaint yourself with your vibration each day. Marvel at the energy that is there and the frequency that's produced.

These secrets are yours to explore, to nurture, to share.

We, as artists, define our times. This time is yours.

REFLECTIONS

What does energy mean to you as it relates to your voice?
    What does frequency mean to you as it relates to your voice?
    What does vibration mean to you as it relates to your voice?
    How can you combine these concepts more vividly in your craft?

What Is in the Control of Craft?

In my experience, there are the three crucial aspects of the artist who wants to pursue/is pursuing a career:

Talent. Craft. Mindset.

Let's just agree that the business, no matter what area of the business you are pursuing, is not fair, needs change, and is, frankly, a dumpster fire most of the time. Let's take it out of the equation for a moment.

What can you, the artist, the performer, control? I suggest three major areas:

The development of your talent.

The craft that allows you to reveal that talent fully and authentically.

The mindset that can make or break you as you navigate the minefield called show business.

This also brings up the idea of "professionalism". Being paid doesn't necessarily make you a professional, and making a choice to work for a community theater doesn't make you automatically an amateur. This is about mindset.

Mindset is the driving force under your talent, your development of craft, and how you move into your career - at whatever level it is.

Mindset allows you to see your talent and seek out what you need to develop it to its fullest. It allows you permission to create and develop craft. It allows you to see your patterns, and to acknowledge your emotional and psychological intelligence. Mindset shows you how to claim these and gives you permission to change.

Mindset affects attitude, self-talk, and motivation. It can induce self-sabotage and crippling self-doubt, but it also can allow you freedom to explore, to release, to learn, and to behave and respond in a way that is healthy, open, and available.

There are just as many unprofessional mindsets trying to pursue a career as there are professional mindsets in community theater. Mindset is everything.

So, what is the magic here? Choice.

And what is the sabotage of mindset? Excuses.

You can choose to be professional in your attitude with yourself. You can choose to pursue excellence and craft. You can choose to develop your talent. You can choose the behavior. You can choose how you speak to yourself. You can choose to acknowledge how the business is a pain in the ass (and do your work anyway).

You can also choose to walk away if you aren't feeling it, aren't aligned with it, or don't want it anymore. You can choose to move in another direction.

You can also choose to make excuses or dramatic declarations; and you can choose to believe them, or not.

Choice isn't success or failure. Choice is choice. It's in your control.

Mindset can create momentum, or it can completely debilitate you. One is a professional mindset; one is not.

Even that is a choice. If you can see the difference, then you can change it.

So, if the magic is to choose, then make it count. And if it's not the choice you want, then change the choice.

Are the most talented people working all the time? No. Is talent the entire picture? Absolutely not.

Are you aware of what you need? Are you aware of what the business is doing? Do you recognize what you need to do? Do you recognize your mindset? Do you know you have the power to change that if it's getting in your way?

Doubt, dry spells, a time of walking through the desert, are all part of the artist's journey as they pursue a career choice. Are you willing to find the professional mindset to navigate that? What are you willing to do to stay the course? To change the course? To be the change?

Seek your level. Know your level. Rise to your level. Begin there. Discover what you have, where you are, and what you need to do in order to change. There's nothing more disappointing than undeveloped potential - in talent, craft, and mindset.

If you want change, be the change. Seek the mindset you wish to have; the one you know you need to have to find the success you pursue. Let that mindset balance with the talent and the craft you are given and are striving to develop and reveal.

The mindset then begins to help to create a place for you: A place that is unique to you and what you have to offer, what you can do, what you can say with your talent and your craft.

Seek to see it. Acknowledge it. Make the changes to align the talent and craft and mindset. It's up to you, and only you.

REFLECTIONS

What am I currently doing to nurture & elevate my talent?

What can I put in place over the next few months to elevate my talent?

How am I currently embodying my craft?

What can I put in place over the next few months to develop my craft further?

What has sabotaged my mindset lately?

What can I do to change that mindset immediately?

What boundaries do I have in place, or need to put in place to feel safe to explore?

What Ever Happened to Craft?

I simply ask - what about craft?

The business of show - from opera to musical theater to theater to tv/film to voiceover - is simply oversaturated. Some are actually talented, some are not. Some have actually studied, some have not. Some have actually developed craft, some have definitely not.

I just see too many resumes with "industry" type classes and not enough actual study of the craft classes. To me, this is simply ass-backwards.

Industry classes present you with a door. As a singer/actor, if you don't have the tools to walk through that door, you are wasting everybody's time.

The tools are the craft, not the game, not the hype, not the brand. You cannot find your brand, your type, your marketing until the truth is in working order. The truth is simply craft, technique, knowledge, and the ability to access it, develop it, and draw on it without hesitation.

How can you create a brand if you haven't studied the craft of your discipline enough to inhabit it fully?

Those that start with the packaging and fake their way into the room will begin to be exposed as surely as those that bring something real and truthful and present that!

The hype and the game expose itself when the resume is set on the table and there is no craft or discipline represented. All you have to do is open your mouth, and we know if the hype is larger than the talent, or the brand is more aggressive than the craft.

If you want to really find your brand/your type, you will drop the hype and the game and simply pursue your craft and your technique with the talent you hold. The stronger your ability to understand and inhabit your craft, the more obvious your brand and your type become.

Often it will even give you options!!!! In fact, dare I say, brand and type become unnecessary, because your authenticity is larger than all that.

What do you need? The desire to be where you are and discover what you have. You need to pursue craft with passion. You need to find out what your instrument can do, - and what you need to do to get it to a place to inhabit it fully and luxuriously!

You need patience, you need focus, you need honesty with yourself.

When the truth of craft is a living, breathing part of you, the game and hype are unnecessary. You give yourself choices as to how you want to be seen in the industry.

None of this is instant. Surprise!!! If you want real, you gotta work for it. If you want instant, you'll get a whole lot of nothing. The packaging might be interesting, shocking, and may catch someone's eye, but once you go back after the double take and begin to unravel it, there had better be craft and technique behind it, otherwise, we are disappointed, and bored.

However, if you dare to work from the inside out and actually build craft, build technique, discover who you are and how your talent blossoms with the craft of discovery, you don't have to be fake and shiny to get noticed.

It is hard to show more when there is nothing there, or you are simply a one-trick pony.

So, even though the industry classes are bright and shiny, and we need them, ask yourself if you are ready to be seen there yet. If you haven't begun your journey as an emerging, discovering artist, you have nothing yet to show. Be seen when you know there is craft you can rely on and a reputation you want to build on. Being told you have "potential" is fine at the beginning. If you aren't developing that potential and are still being told you have potential, or HAD potential, that's a big ouch.

Find the substance first - create it, mold it, and know it is an ongoing journey. The icing of discovering where it will be best molded happens when that journey is well on its way!

REFLECTIONS

What does potential mean to me?

What have I realized and developed and inhabited about my potential now?

Where do I hope to grow that potential?

How do I see that growth? What am I willing to do to embrace that growth of potential?

Postlude
Play!

Remember play? Let's not forget it. In our pursuit of craft, of career, of getting it "right," we forget the childlike qualities of play.

Play allows for curiosity, for exploration.

Play can be self-directed. It can be intrinsically motivated. It can have a mental stimulus that is physically active. It can be imaginative.

Play can't take itself too seriously. It's not about right or wrong, good, or bad, perfection or imperfection. It's not about value judgment.

Play is just... Play.

Perhaps this is the hardest thing of all. Allowing ourselves to play. Letting ourselves move, make sound, paint outside the lines, without stopping or correcting anything. Just enjoying what happens is hard - and yet is the most freeing.

Perhaps it's time to re-discover the play in your creative life. Reclaim the joy for the sake of the joy, for the sake of the doing, for the sake of the curiosity, for the sake of how it makes you feel on all levels of consciousness.

If we take ourselves too seriously, we lose the play. We lose the wonder. We forget why we are doing all of this in the first place.

There is always more to do. First, let's play.

REFLECTIONS

How can you add more play in your life?

Just sing through ONE SONG WITHOUT STOPPING this week. Make mistakes. Laugh. Sing. Just sing.

Create a new playlist of songs that simply make you want to sing!!

Glitter & Unicorn Poop

"It's a terrible thing, I think, in life to wait until you're ready. I have this feeling now that actually no one is ever ready to do anything. There is almost no such thing as ready. There is only now. And you may as well do it now. Generally speaking, now is as good a time as any." - Hugh Laurie

Craft is craft is craft. Lack of craft is lack of craft. If you say you are a singer, then you must sing. If you say you are a XYZ/fill in the blank, then you must do that thing.

Glitter and unicorn poop can't save you.

I wish my personal trainer had glitter and unicorn poop. Then I could magically just get rid of those extra pounds I want to lose and give me Michelle Obama arms. If I think going into the gym once is going to achieve this, I need to change my mindset. (Just to be clear, I don't think it to be true, but I WISH it were true!)

I have to commit to what the work is. I have to acknowledge the mindset and claim it, so I can make a plan I can focus on and stick to. And then I have to do the work.

See where I am going?

When you are ready to do the work, and choose the work, then the mindset changes. This is rather simultaneous. The mindset, the spirit, the focus creates the change for you to find the structure to build and develop the technical behavior, the athleticism, and the craft. Having a "nice voice" isn't enough. It's never been enough. Striving for the craft to allow you to do the work you desire demands all of your parts!

So, ask some questions: What do I want? Do I want that now? If yes, what do I need to do in order to be ready for now? What will that take?

What is reasonable? Am I setting up goals that I can achieve in the short term? Long term? Am I creating pitfalls and sabotage? Who can I trust (or learn to trust) to guide me, teach me, coach me to become better than my previous self, as a human being and as an artist? What does my technical behavior need now? What does my craft need? Where do I begin?

All these questions can be overwhelming at once, so take it easy, one at a time.

It all comes from the inside; the core of your being, of breath, of voice; the core of your determination and focus.

Glitter and unicorn poop might create the illusion of magic, but after a while it's going to get messy and annoying, and that glitter is stuck to everything forever.

The true magic is in the process and the journey you create moving into that truth. The true magic of that process reveals itself as you create: yourself, your craft, your path, your play.

When you are ready, it starts with YOU. You are simply enough. You are the magic.

Create yourself. Claim the authenticity, claim the technique, claim the craft, claim the mindset. Claim it all. No more excuses. No more hesitations. No more.

It's yours if you dare to lean in and see it reflected back to you. Reach for it and grab that brass ring.

Claim beyond the technique.

It is yours to sculpt and breathe life into. Every single day.

FINAL REFLECTIONS

What do I truly want in my life? What are the big themes?

What do I want in my artistic life RIGHT NOW?

What am I ready and able to DO right now?

What am I needing to do to find these realities?

What am I willing to do to build technique, craft & mindset?

Who do I trust, who do I have or need on my team?

Who do I need to have on my team that isn't there?

Where do I begin, TODAY?

What does my next chapter look like?

About the author

Susan Eichhorn Young

Susan's journey has led her to teach & create theater worldwide. Her mission to help others access authenticity and support performers & artists to discover & reveal their authentic voice, has given her a platform in the private studio, as a voice consultant, collaborator, as a clinician in masterclasses & workshops, as an adjudicator, and in her online presence.

Her diverse clientele encompasses emerging artists to established & award-winning artists in theater, music theater, cabaret, opera, tv & film.

Located in New York City, her innovative approach has generated a thriving studio which keeps her in high demand within both the Broadway & Operatic communities.

Now, due to technology, Susan is able to work & consult with singers & actors, directors & theater companies around the globe via online platforms, as well as in person.

Teacher, mentor, singer, actor, writer, speaker - Susan embraces these demanding disciplines with passion, an ongoing pursuit of knowledge, humanity & a little laughter.

Her renowned blog is read worldwide, and this and all her online courses can be found on her website: susaneichhornyoung.com.

www.ingramcontent.com/pod-product-compliance
Lightning Source LLC
Chambersburg PA
CBHW050528170426
43201CB00013B/2129